Your Stomach

by Anne Ylvisaker

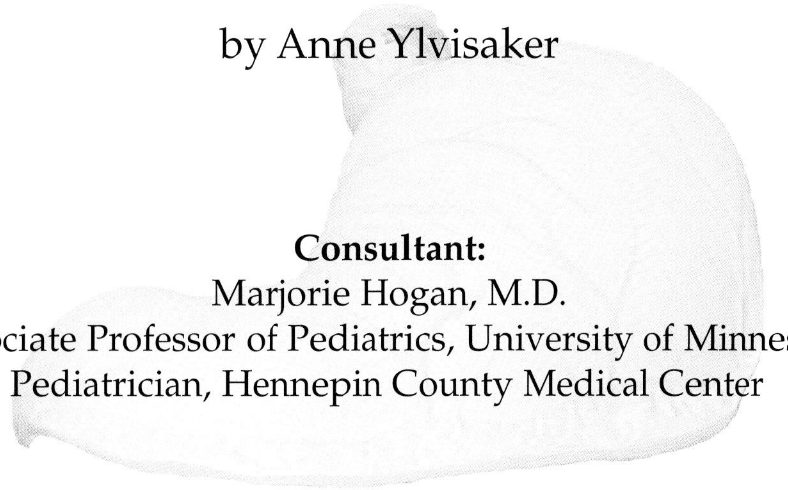

Consultant:
Marjorie Hogan, M.D.
Associate Professor of Pediatrics, University of Minnesota
Pediatrician, Hennepin County Medical Center

Bridgestone Books
an imprint of Capstone Press
Mankato, Minnesota

Bridgestone Books are published by Capstone Press
151 Good Counsel Drive, P.O. Box 669, Mankato, Minnesota 56002
http://www.capstone-press.com

Library of Congress Cataloging-in-Publication Data
Ylvisaker, Anne.
Your stomach / by Anne Ylvisaker.
    p. cm.—(Bridgestone science library)
    Includes bibliographical references and index.
    Summary: A simple introduction to the stomach, including its makeup, function
within the digestive system, stomach diseases, and how to keep your stomach healthy.
ISBN 0-7368-1151-6
1. Stomach—Juvenile literature. [1. Stomach. 2. Digestion. 3. Digestive system.] I. Title.
II. Series.
QP151 .Y59 2002
612.3'2—dc21

2001003591

Editorial Credits
Rebecca Glaser, editor; Karen Risch, product planning editor; Linda Clavel, cover and
    interior layout designer and illustrator; Alta Schaffer, photo researcher; Nancy White,
    photo stylist

Photo Credits
Capstone Press/Gary Sundermeyer, cover (all), 1, 16, 18, 20
G. Shih-R. Kessel/Visuals Unlimited, 14
Unicorn Stock Photos/Tom, Dee Ann McCarthey, 4

**Bridgestone Books thanks South Central Technical College, North Mankato, Minnesota,
for providing medical models used in photos.**

Table of Contents

Your Stomach

Your stomach is an organ made of muscle. It lies just below your ribs. Your stomach stores food and begins breaking it down. Food must be broken down so that its nutrients can go into your body. Your body needs nutrients for energy.

nutrient
something that people need to stay healthy and strong; nutrients come from food.

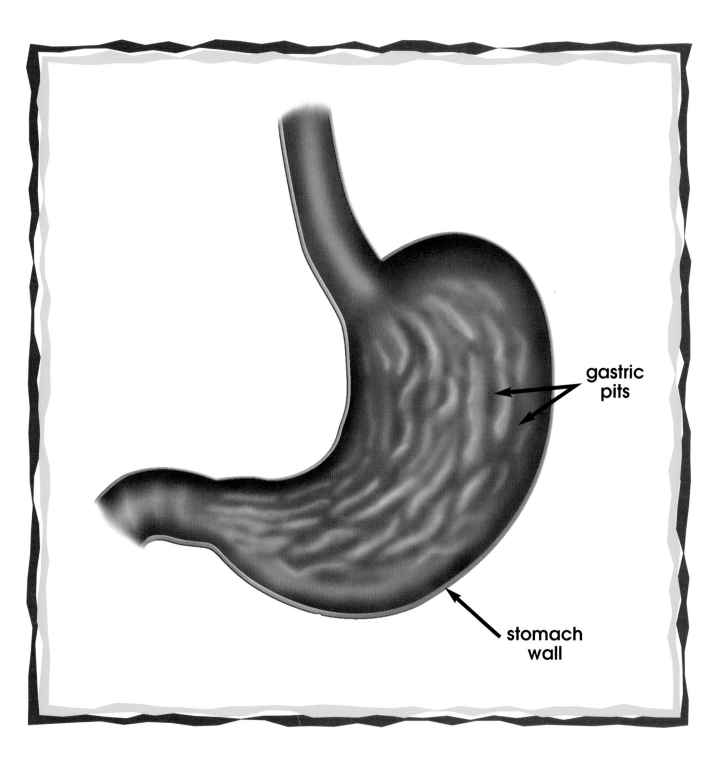

gastric
pits

stomach
wall

Inside Your Stomach

Your stomach is shaped like the letter J. It is about the size of your two fists. Stomach walls are made of muscle. Gastric pits line the stomach wall. These openings let gastric juices into the stomach. The juices break down food.

gastric
having to do with
the stomach

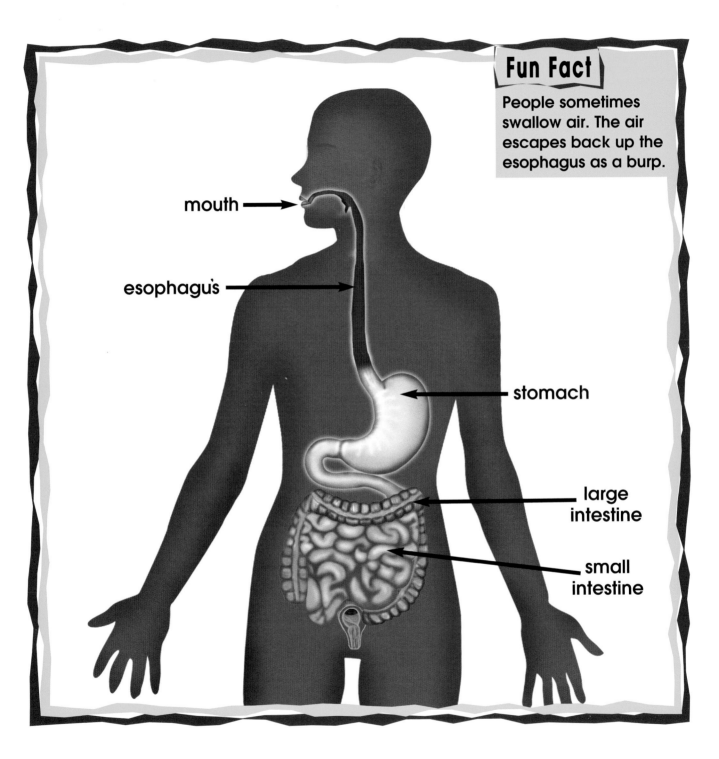

Fun Fact

People sometimes swallow air. The air escapes back up the esophagus as a burp.

mouth

esophagus

stomach

large intestine

small intestine

Your Digestive System

Your digestive system breaks down food so your body can use it. The mouth, esophagus (e-SOF-uh-guhss), stomach, and intestines are the main parts of the digestive system. The digestive system also gets rid of food parts that your body cannot use.

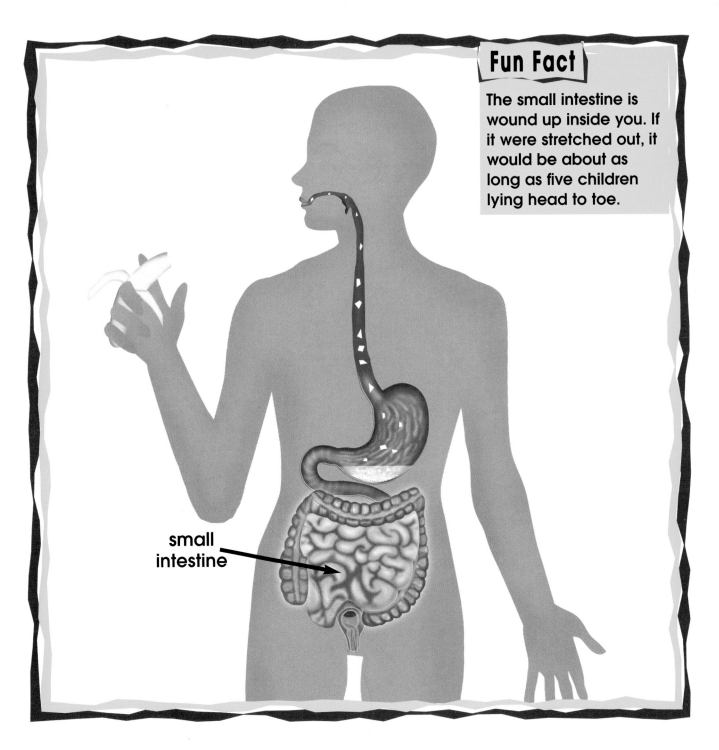

small
intestine

What Happens When You Eat?

When you chew, saliva mixes with the food. The food forms a small ball. When you swallow, the food ball goes down your esophagus. Muscles in this tube squeeze the food down to your stomach.

saliva

the clear liquid in your mouth that helps you swallow and begin to digest food

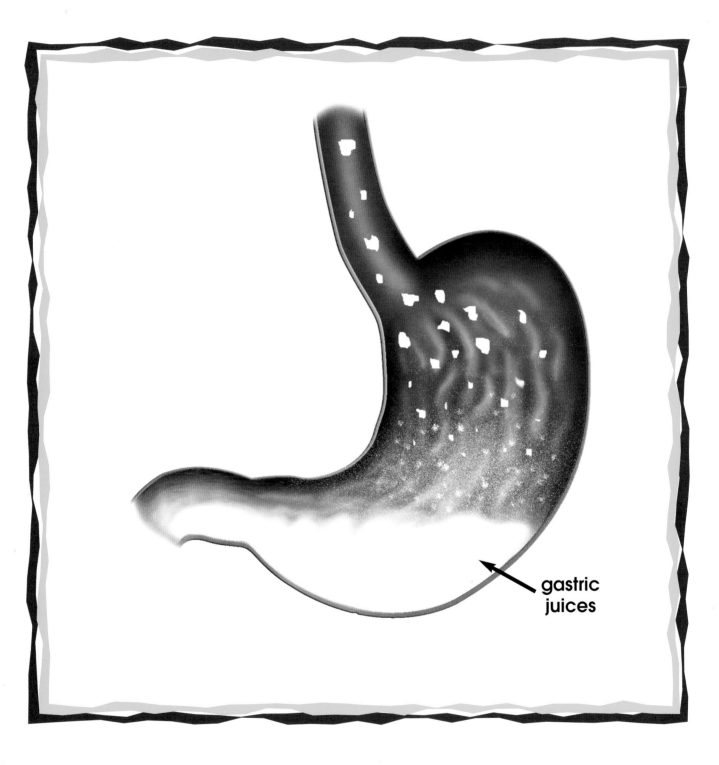

gastric
juices

What Happens Inside Your Stomach?

In your stomach, the food mixes with gastric juices. The gastric juices break the food ball into smaller pieces. The muscles of the stomach walls squeeze the food pieces. Finally, the food pieces turn into liquid. The liquid then flows into the small intestine.

This picture shows villi magnified 140 times.

Inside Your Intestines

In the small intestine, villi take nutrients from the digested food. The villi pass nutrients into the blood. Your body cannot use all parts of food. The leftover parts go to the large intestine. The large intestine pushes leftover food out of your body through the anus.

villi

tiny growths in the small intestine that absorb nutrients

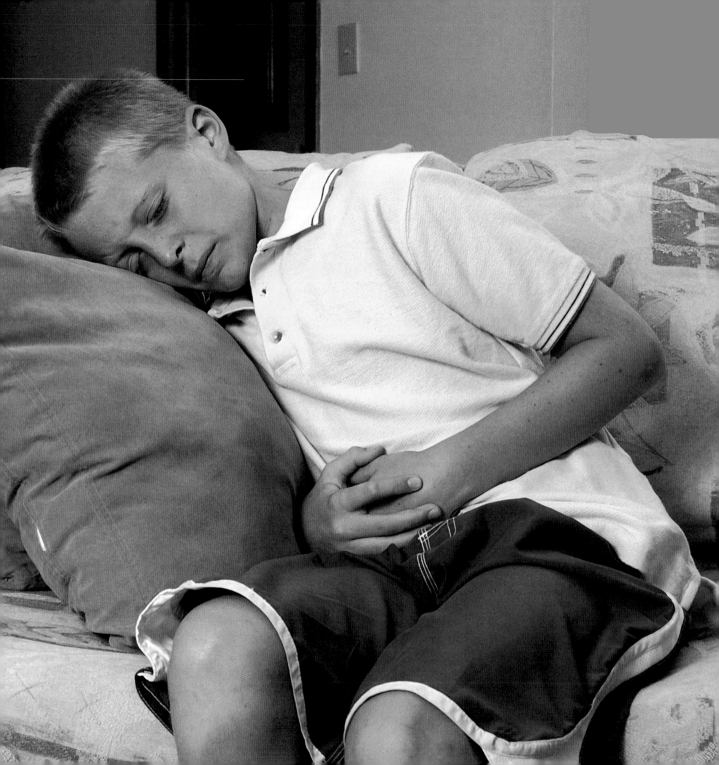

Feeling Full

When your stomach is full, it sends a
message to your brain. The message
tells you to stop eating. Your stomach
will hurt if you keep eating. The pain
is your stomach muscles squeezing
together. If you eat too much, your
body stores the extra food energy as fat.

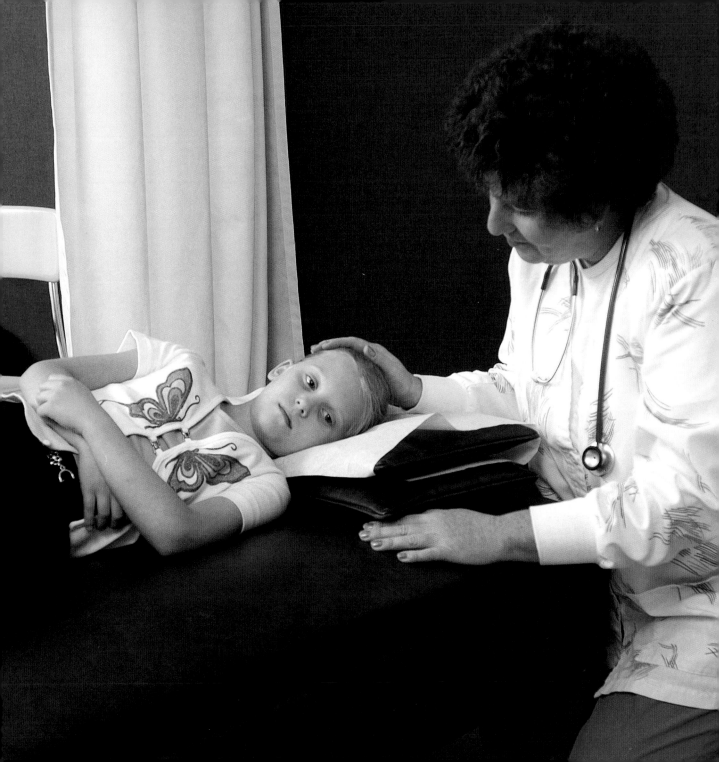

Feeling Sick to Your Stomach

Your stomach can feel sick for several reasons. You might have the flu. Ulcers are sores in the stomach or the intestines caused by bacteria. Constipation happens when food moves too slowly through the intestines. Fiber helps relieve constipation.

bacteria
single-celled creatures that can cause sickness

A Healthy Stomach

You can keep your stomach healthy. Germs that cause sickness may be on your food or hands. Wash fruits and vegetables before you eat them. Eat high-fiber foods such as bread or fruit. Fiber helps food move smoothly through your digestive system.

germ

a living cell that can cause sickness

21

Hands On: Why Does Your Stomach Growl?

You may hear your stomach rumble or growl when you are hungry. Try this activity to find out why.

What You Need

2 round balloons
Sink
An adult to help

What You Do

1. Ask an adult to help you fill one balloon with water. Stretch the balloon over the water faucet and hold the balloon there.
2. Turn on the water slowly. Hold the bottom of the balloon.
3. Turn the water off when the balloon is about 6 inches (15 centimeters) wide. Take the balloon off the faucet and tie it closed.
4. Blow up the other balloon with air and tie it closed. It should be about the same size as the water balloon.
5. Lightly squeeze and rub your fingers over each balloon. Which one makes a louder noise?

The balloons are like your stomach. The empty balloon makes a louder noise. Your stomach rumbles more loudly when it is empty. The noises come from your muscles squeezing air. The water balloon is like your stomach when you are full. The stomach muscles squeeze the food.

Words to Know

anus (AY-nuhs)—the lower opening of the digestive system; solid wastes move out of the body through the anus

esophagus (e-SOF-uh-guhss)—the tube that carries food from the throat to the stomach

fiber (FYE-bur)—a part of foods such as bread and fruit that passes through the body but is not digested; fiber helps food move through the intestines.

gastric (GASS-trik)—having to do with the stomach

liquid (LIK-wid)—a wet substance that flows into the shape of its container

nutrient (NOO-tree-uhnt)—something that people need to stay strong and healthy; nutrients are found in food.

saliva (suh-LYE-vuh)—the clear liquid in your mouth that helps you swallow and begin to digest food

Read More

Cromwell, Sharon. *Why Does My Tummy Rumble When I'm Hungry?: and Other Questions about the Digestive System.* Body Wise. Des Plaines, Ill.: Rigby Interactive Library, 1998.

Maynard, Jacqui. *I Know Where My Food Goes.* Sam's Science. Cambridge, Mass.: Candlewick Press, 1999.

Showers, Paul. *What Happens to a Hamburger?* Let's Read and Find Out Science. New York: HarperCollins, 2001.

Internet Sites

The Digestive System
http://tqjunior.thinkquest.org/5777/dig1.htm?tqskip=1
The Real Deal on the Digestive System
http://www.kidshealth.org/kid/body/digest_noSW.html
Your Gross and Cool Body—Digestive System
http://yucky.kids.discovery.com/flash/body/pg000126.html

Index